violin

ACKNOWLEDGEMENTS

Thanks SO MUCH to: Tom Yardley for the recording;
Jane Dawson for the photographs; Anthony Dawson
for the computer!; Olly Cox (percussion); Bruno Heinen
(keyboard); and Henrik (double bass and bass guitar);
Ben Dawson for the driving; Ben Hancox, Robin
Ashwell and Cara Berridge for being cool; my family.

Printed in the United Kingdom by
MPG Books Ltd, Bodmin

Published by SMT, an imprint of
Sanctuary Publishing Limited
Sanctuary House
45–53 Sinclair Road
London W14 0NS
United Kingdom

www.sanctuarypublishing.com

Picture Credits: Rex Features, Redferns,
Getty Images and Kelly Clark Fotography.
Design and Editorial: Essential Works

ISBN: 1-84492-037-2

XTREME

violin

Hannah Dawson

smt

CONTENTS

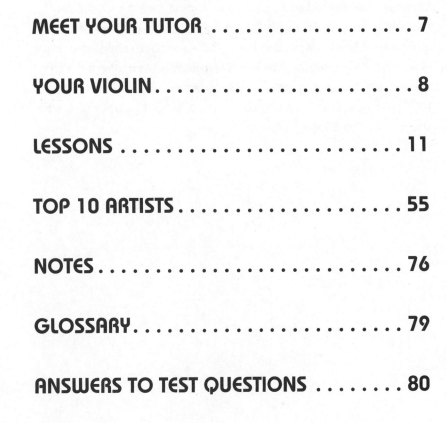

INTRODUCTION

Welcome to *Xtreme Violin*, the book that's going to get you off
to an amazing start on the fabulous fiddle! There's going to be a
lot to take in, but the good thing about this book is that you can
read it again and again, and take as much time as you like! The
violin is notoriously difficult, so don't be too hard on yourself.
Through a series of ten lessons, you should develop the skills
to be able to take off in no time! There are also profiles of ten
amazing violinists. You will be able to learn about them, and even
how to imitate their styles! Don't forget, the CD at the front of
the book is full of exercises and pieces that you can play along
to. So, let me introduce you to Bowie, who will be your guide for
the rest of the book…

MEET YOUR TUTOR

TRACK 1

BOWIE IS HERE TO GUIDE YOU...

'Hey... Wassup?! My name's Bowie and I'm going to be guiding you through ten sweet lessons in playing the violin. We're going to have a wicked time, just you wait and see. And in no time you'll be playing like me!

You know what? You have chosen the best instrument of the lot. Soon people will be singing, smiling, dancing and grooving to the funky tunes you'll play. Now I promise you I'm going to make this as painless as possible. So, no yawning allowed... OK?'

ADVISE YOU...

'The violin is used in so many styles of music. Hopefully my lessons will help you decide what kind of music inspires you to play the violin. There are some wicked pop songs you might know which have really funky violin solos in them, for example: "Penny Lane" (The Beatles) and "Bittersweet Symphony" (The Verve).'

TEST YOU...

'If you wanna be a hot fiddler, I'm afraid there's going to be some theory along the way. Don't worry, I won't get too heavy 'cos I want this to be fun for the both of us!

At the end of each lesson, I'm going to test you on the things that we've covered. You'll find the answers at the back of the book.'

MAKE YOU LAUGH...

'My first really important gig was with my band at the Shepherds Bush Empire in London. We'd been rehearsing for ages and we were all really excited about playing at such a wicked venue. However, when I was getting ready to go on stage, I realised I'd left my bow at home! I was so embarrassed – I had to pluck my strings for the whole gig! My band never let me live it down and they nicknamed me "Bowie"!'

YOUR VIOLIN

The violin is an amazing instrument and has been around for centuries. It hasn't really changed at all in all these years but there are a few bits and pieces that people have added to make it all a bit more comfortable! This diagram shows you some of the most important parts of the violin.

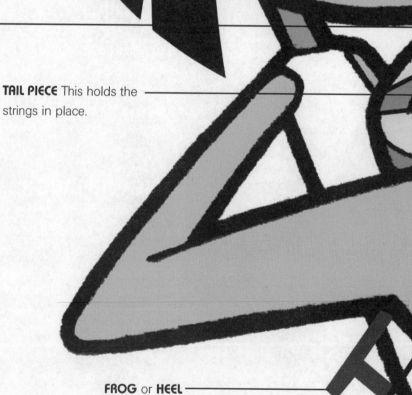

BRIDGE This holds the strings up so they don't touch the fingerboard. When you play your violin, vibrations pass from the bridge to the soundpost (positioned inside the violin). The soundwaves then escape through the 'f' holes.

TAIL PIECE This holds the strings in place.

FROG or **HEEL**

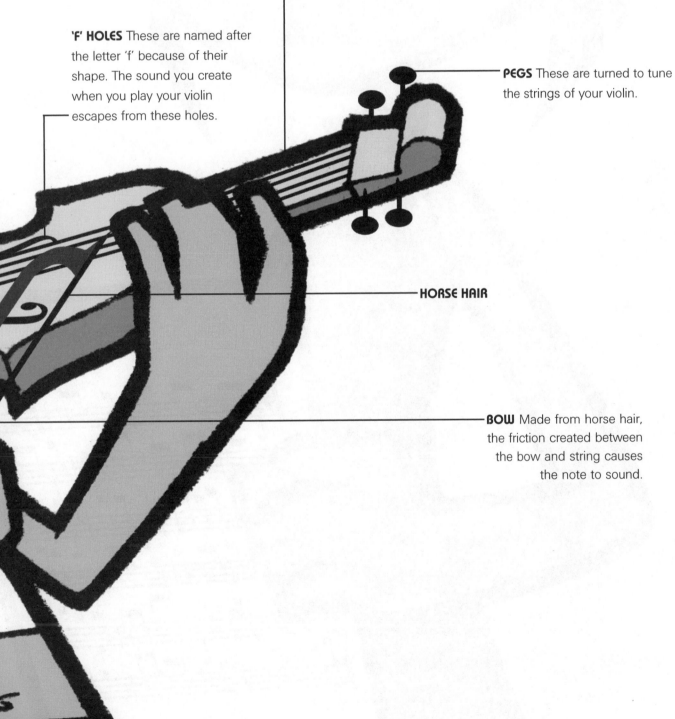

FINGERBOARD Depressing the string against the fingerboard changes the length of the string and therefore the pitch.

'F' HOLES These are named after the letter 'f' because of their shape. The sound you create when you play your violin escapes from these holes.

PEGS These are turned to tune the strings of your violin.

HORSE HAIR

BOW Made from horse hair, the friction created between the bow and string causes the note to sound.

LESSONS

POSTURE, POSITION AND NAMES OF STRINGS

Before you even play a note on the violin, it's really important that you're standing or sitting properly. It can be quite tiring work, so if you're not comfortable, you're not going to make the best possible sound. Get into good habits now, and you'll find playing a whole lot easier!

YOUR GOALS

GOAL 1
To be able to hold your violin in a comfortable position while standing or sitting.

GOAL 2
To be able to name each of the strings.

GOAL 3
To be able to pluck the strings with your right-hand fingers.

THEORY

If you wanna be a classy fiddler, you've gotta be able to look and feel cool with this funky new tool!

Correct playing position when standing

Correct playing position when seated

IN PRACTICE

STEP 1

Stand with your feet about 20cm apart, with your toes slightly turned outwards. Make sure that you feel well balanced and that your knee joints are nicely relaxed.

STEP 2

Hold your violin by the neck with your left hand, take the chin rest with your right hand and gently guide it to rest on your left shoulder, along your collarbone, with the side of your jaw gently resting on the chin rest.

STEP 3

You do not need to use your left hand until Lesson 4, so you can just use it to gently support the violin by holding it like this:

STEP 4

Now you can try plucking the strings. In music, when a composer requests string players to pluck the string, they write the Italian term for plucking, 'pizzicato'.

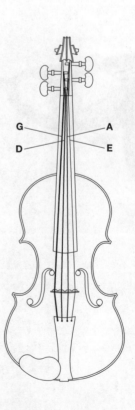

Anchor your right thumb under the right end of the fingerboard, and use the fleshy part of your index finger to pluck the strings about 2cm from the end of the fingerboard. (You can also do this without your thumb as an anchor. Experiment with plucking the string within a circular motion made through the air – this can make a more resonant sound.)

Each of your violin strings has its own name. The thickest string makes the lowest sound and is called the G string. Each of the strings are labeled in the diagram on the right:

TUNING YOUR VIOLIN

Each of your strings should match the sound of the corresponding notes on the keyboard. Your G string should match the sound of the G below Middle C on the keyboard. (If you don't have a keyboard, you can buy tuning pipes that produce the notes that each of your strings should be tuned to.) The diagram below shows which piano keys relate to the strings on the violin.

Middle C

Your violin will definitely have 'tuning pegs', but it might also have 'adjusters' on all the strings (or perhaps just on the E string). Tune each string by using either of these mechanisms. (The adjusters are more suitable for fine tuning – if the string is only a tiny bit out of tune.) Pluck each string individually and then play the corresponding note on the piano. It might be, for example, that the G string on your violin sounds higher than the G below Middle C on the piano. If this is the case, follow these simple steps:

STEP 1

Sit down and support the chin-rest end of your violin on your right thigh and hold the neck of your violin with your right hand. (The front of your violin should be facing you.)

STEP 2

Gently turn the peg towards your body a tiny bit. (You might have to push it in slightly at the same time, towards the scroll, to stop it from unraveling.)

STEP 3

Pluck the string and then play the G on the piano to determine whether the two sounds match. If the notes do match, the string is in tune, and you can try to tune the next string. If they don't match, and the note is still too high, turn the peg again, slightly towards you. If it is too low, turn the peg away from you.

(If you do have adjusters, and if the string is only slightly out of tune, turn the adjuster clockwise if you want to make the string sound higher or 'sharper', and anti-clockwise if you want it to sound lower or 'flatter'.)

Continue this process with each of the strings. Remember, if the pitch of the note is sharper than it should be, turn your peg away from you. If it is flatter than it should be, turn it towards you.

The pegs and adjusters are purely mechanisms that alter the 'length' of your violin strings. The longer the string is, the sharper the pitch will sound. The shorter the string is, the flatter the pitch will sound.

PROBLEM?

Because you are new to the violin and it's new to you, you might find it tiring holding it for a long time. Don't worry, this will soon pass if you practise with a good posture. There's no harm in stopping if it starts to hurt, and returning when you feel refreshed!

TIP

Stretch your body before you start; it will improve your playing and work that heart.

EXERCISES

All the exercises in this lesson are to be plucked. Listen to the CD: each of the exercises will consist of me playing (you can play along, too). Then, on the repeat, play along to the beat!

1. I have written the names of the strings that I want you to play. Try and follow the music and pluck the strings in the order I have written them. There will be four beats before you come in; pluck the strings on each beat.

2. This exercise is to be plucked as well. Again, pluck the strings in the order that I have written them.

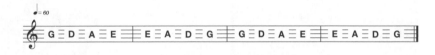

3. This is the final plucking exercise.

TEST

QUESTION 1
What is the name of the highest string on the violin?

QUESTION 2
What is the Italian word for plucking?

QUESTION 3
Which way should you turn your peg if your string is sounding too low ('flat')?

THE BOW

The bow's the one who's got the flow, don't you know? So, let's give it a go... give it up for the bow!

YOUR GOALS

GOAL 1
To be able to hold the bow properly.

GOAL 2
To understand how the bow produces sound from the violin.

THEORY

Here's a bit of bow info:

The best wood for a violin bow is taken from the 'pernambuco' tree. This wood is naturally resilient and reddish-brown in colour. The hair for a bow is taken from a horse's tail. We rub 'rosin' (used to be a sticky block of resin made from the sap from a tree! Now it's made from the distillation of oil of turpentine) gently on the horsehair to give it a coating of sticky residue: this produces friction when the bow is rubbed against the strings. This friction causes the strings to vibrate.

Two different perspectives of a good bow hold:

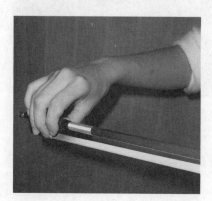
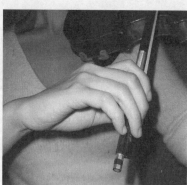

IN PRACTICE

STEP 1

Hold the stick of your bow carefully in the middle with your left
hand. Shake your right hand gently up and down to ensure that
it is relaxed. Put your right thumb in the gap between the stick
and the frog.

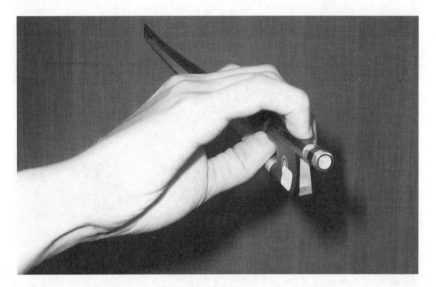

Let your fingers curl naturally over the stick, with your third finger
opposite your thumb. Let your index finger rest next to your
middle fingers (make sure there is a bit of space between each
of the fingers). Rest the tip of your little (fourth) finger on the
stick. You can try moving the bow up and down by pressing your
little finger up and down. (You can practice this at any time with
a pencil instead of your bow!)

STEP 2

A 'down-bow' is when the direction of the bow moves from the
heel to the tip. Make sure that your bow hold is still good and
try placing the bow hair at the heel of the bow on the E string.
Guide the bow downwards towards the tip, making sure that
it stays in a straight line (at right angles to the bridge and the
fingerboard). To do an 'up-bow', guide the bow back towards
the heel, maintaining a good bow hold and still keeping the
bow at a right angle to the bridge.

TIP

It is very important that your bow-hand is as relaxed as possible. Take an imaginary paintbrush in your right hand and paint an invisible wall, up and down. Notice how fluid the motion is. You should try to achieve this type of motion when you use your bow.

To play each of the different strings, your elbow should be at different places. To play the G string, it should be at its highest point. Here are photos of the two different arm positions when you bow…

… the E string

… the G string

PROBLEM?

You might find that sometimes you produce unpleasant sounds. This might be because you are bowing too near the bridge. Experiment with putting your bow in different places across the strings. When you are playing a piece of music on the violin, you need to be ready to adjust the sound depending on what mood you want to convey (eg to play really quietly, you need to move your bow nearer the fingerboard).

EXERCISE

In these exercises, I will direct you to use different parts of the bow. Below is a diagram of the names of these different parts.

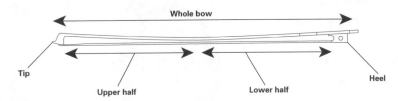

A down-bow is shown on a piece of music, like this:

and an up-bow, like this: ∨

Sometimes, composers might direct you to play a more articulated stroke which bounces off the string. This is called 'staccato' in Italian. When they want this, they usually write a dot below or above the note.

1. Play this first exercise with the lower half of the bow. Before you begin, make sure that your bow hold is good and that you are not tense. As you play, watch your bow and make sure that it is always moving at right angles with the bridge. This will minimise any scratchy sounds!

2. This next exercise is to be played on the upper half of the bow.

3. This exercise is for practising repeated down-bows. To play the same bow more than once (eg two down-bows) is called 'retaking'. Play these with the lower half of the bow.

4. You can use the whole bow for this exercise.

TRACK 4 CD

TRACK 5 CD

TRACK 6 CD

TRACK 7 CD

TEST

QUESTION 1

What is the name we give when the bow moves from the heel to the tip?

QUESTION 2

What is the name of the most suitable wood for making bows?

QUESTION 3

What is the name of the substance that we rub on our bows to produce friction?

RHYTHMS

The rhythm on the street
Is to a funky beat
You can dance
You can sing
You just do your thing

YOUR GOALS

GOAL 1
To recognise note values.

GOAL 2
To be able to read rhythms and play them on your violin.

THEORY

You know what? You're about to learn about such a cool thing. The funny thing is, you already know about it 'cos it's all around you – speech has rhythm, nature has rhythm, even mechanical objects have rhythm.

Rhythm is just as important in music as the notes are. If you play a well-known tune with vague note-values, it becomes meaningless.

This note table is a simple way to explain different note values.

NOTE	REST	UK NAME	US NAME
o	▬	semi-breve or semi-breve rest	whole note or whole-note rest
♩	▬	minim or minim rest	half note or half-note rest
♩	𝄽	crotchet or crotchet rest	quarter note or quarter-note rest
♪	𝄾	quaver or quaver rest	eighth note or eighth-note rest
♬	𝄿	semi-quaver or semi-quaver rest	16th note or 16th-note rest

These are the most important note values for you to learn at the beginning. This table tells you the names of all the note values and rests (silences) that you will use in this book.

In the note table, the note that lasts the longest amount of time is the semi-breve. As you go down the table, the notes are halved in length. Or you could say, as you work upwards, the notes are doubled in length!

IN PRACTICE

A good way of explaining rhythms is by using a song that you will definitely know. Sorry, it's not very cool, but I think it might come in useful: 'Baa Baa Black Sheep'!

STEP 1

This song uses a combination of crotchets, quavers and minims. You can play this along to the CD. You only need to use the A-string for this one. Do you remember the words? Here they are just in case you need them:

'Baa baa black sheep, have you any wool?
Yes Sir, yes Sir, three bags full.
One for the Master and one for the Dame,
And one for the little boy who lives down the lane!'

STEP 2

Now try playing this rhythm using all four strings:

STEP 3

Another way to practice rhythms on your violin is to invent your own. One way of doing this is by converting sentences into rhythms on your violin. Think of a type of food/drink and a famous person/band and say it out loud as if you were rapping. For example, 'I ate chocolate cake, with Justin Timberlake'. Now think it in your head and play it on one string of your violin!

Wicked… you're starting to sound pretty cool!

STEP 4

Dotted rhythms are just a development of the rhythms in your note table. If you add a dot to the right-hand side of a note, then it adds on half as much again.

Here is another note table, but this time it shows you the value of dotted notes.

NAME OF NOTE	SYMBOL	FORMULA	SIMPLEST FORM
dotted quaver/eighth note	♪.	♪ + ♪	♪ + ♪ + ♪
dotted crotchet/quarter note	♩.	♩ + ♪	♪ + ♪ + ♪
dotted minim/half note	𝅗𝅥.	𝅗𝅥 + ♩	♩ + ♩ + ♩
dotted semi-breve/whole note	𝅝.	𝅝 + 𝅗𝅥	𝅗𝅥 + 𝅗𝅥 + 𝅗𝅥

Often, dotted notes are followed by semi-quavers/quavers. This kind of rhythm is used a lot in folk music.

PROBLEM?

If you've never learned how to read music before, it might take you a while to get used to all these new terms. Don't let it put you off, though. It's just like learning a language: after a while it will become automatic.

TIP

In each of the musical examples there is a click that will show you the main beats of each piece. This will help you to develop a strong sense of rhythm. To keep things simple, all the exercises and pieces stay the same speed ('tempo') throughout.

EXERCISES

1. This exercise uses all the strings and teaches you how to play one type of dotted rhythm. This one is when a dotted quaver is followed by a semi-quaver. It sounds a bit like the rhythm of a horse galloping.

2. This next exercise teaches you how to play another type of dotted rhythm. This one is opposite to the one in the last exercise. This time the semi-quaver is followed by the dotted semi-quaver.

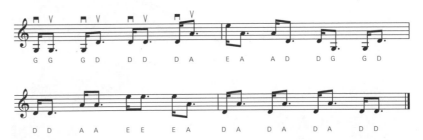

3. This exercise combines the two dotted rhythms that I have shown you. You might find a pattern emerging at the beginning, but watch out – it's not always the same!

TEST

QUESTION 1
What is the name for a silence in music?

QUESTION 2
Can you name three different note values?

READING THOSE DOTS!

Now, this is the final basic step to being able to read music and play it on your violin. You're doing so well, it's just swell!

YOUR GOALS

GOAL 1
To be able to read notes on the violin.

GOAL 2
To develop a good left-hand position.

GOAL 3
To understand how the left hand changes the pitch of the note.

THEORY

Now, you already know that the thicker the string is, the lower the sound it makes. Well, our left hand can alter the pitch of notes as well by making the string shorter/longer. When you place your finger on the string (so it is touching the fingerboard), you are effectively making the string shorter. Have you ever got a rubber band and stretched it over a cardboard box? This is the same principal as a violin and its strings. If you stretch the rubber band, the more taut it is, the higher the pitch is when you pluck it. If you place your finger on the string of your violin, it alters the length of string that is free to vibrate.

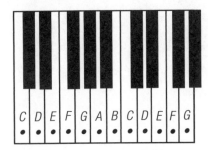

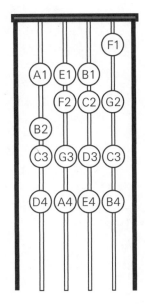

Reading music on the violin is really quite straightforward; you just have to get the hang of it. A good way to help you to understand is by using a keyboard and relating the notes to keys on the piano. Here is a diagram of a keyboard with the names of all of the keys.

In music, we name each note of the scale with a letter of the alphabet: A, B, C, D, E, F, and G. These seven notes make up an 'octave'.

You can play these notes on your violin by placing your fingers on the strings in particular positions. In the diagram on the left, I have marked the positions of the notes on your violin that are equivalent to the white keys on a piano. Each circle is strategically positioned on the appropriate string, and inside each circle is a letter name and a number.

The letter is the name of the note that will sound if you place your finger in that position.

The number is the number of the finger that you can use to play that particular note.

Notice how some of the finger positions are further apart than others (eg between A and B). This is the same on the keyboard: between A and B there is a black key, whereas B and C are right next to each other, without a black key between them. When two white keys on a keyboard have a black key in between them, it means that they are a whole tone apart. B and C on the keyboard don't have a black key between them. This means that they are a semi-tone apart. Each of the black keys on the keyboard can either be a sharp or a flat.

The symbol for a sharp is: ♯

The symbol for a flat is: ♭

If you sharpen a D by a semi-tone, you will have the note D♯. This will be the black key (on the keyboard) to the right of the D.

If you flatten D by a semi-tone, you will have the note D♭. This will be the black key to the left of D.

If you want to play D♯ on your violin, place your finger slightly closer towards you, in-between the positions for the notes D and E.

If you want to play a D♭, place your finger slightly further away from you, in-between the positions for C and D.

READING MUSIC

We write music on a 'stave'. This consists of five parallel lines. Each note of the scale has a fixed place on the stave. If a note is higher or lower in pitch than the stave can accommodate, then we use 'ledger' lines so the notes aren't just floating on the page. Here is a stave with some of the notes that you can play on your violin, starting with the lowest note (your G string). I have put the note's name above the note. Below each note, I have put the string that the note can be played on, and the finger you can use to play that note.

Once you get used to this way of reading/writing music, it will become automatic – like reading a book. I have written in the open strings of your violin and the fingers that correspond to each note on this diagram. Throughout this book, in all the exercises and pieces, I will label the notes with fingerings and names of the string you should be playing (For example, G 3 = third finger on the G string).

IN PRACTICE

STEP 1

Put your first finger on the G string in the place that I have shown in the diagram. Push it down lightly, just enough that the string touches the fingerboard. Make sure that your finger is nice and curved. Let your thumb rest opposite your first and second fingers. (Your thumb should be as relaxed as possible but also help to support the violin. There should always be space between the neck of the violin and your thumb.) Now pluck the G string with your right index finger. (Your left first finger should still be in position. You should have plucked an A. If you have a piano, you can play the A below Middle C to make sure that your finger is in the right place. If the note that you have plucked is too high (compared to the equivalent note on the keyboard), make it flatter by sliding your finger away from you slightly, towards the scroll of your violin. To make it sharper, slide it towards you.

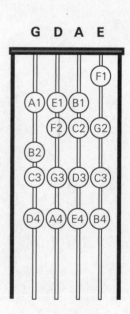

STEP 2

Do the same thing with your second finger. Put it in the second position (a tone away from the first finger and the same distance away from the nut as the first finger is). Now pluck the G string again. You should now have plucked a B.

STEP 3

Now put your third finger in the same place as the diagram shows. This should be a semi-tone away from the second finger, so they should be close together. Pluck this note. It should sound a C.

STEP 4

Put your fourth finger on the fourth position in the diagram. This should be a tone apart from your third finger. Pluck it and a D should sound.

Now, this D is the same note as the next string up (the D string). When you play the violin, you can choose whether you want to use your fourth finger or an open string, depending on the type of sound that you want. It is good to practise using your fourth finger because it can be very useful. It is good to strengthen it from the beginning because it tends to be smaller and weaker than the other fingers.

EXERCISE

1. This exercise introduces your first finger.

G0 G1 G0   D0 E1 D0   A0 A1 A0   E0 F1 E0

2. This exercise uses your first and second fingers. Use the rest in each bar to move your first finger to the next string up.

G1 G2 G1   D1 D2 D1   A1 A2 A1   E1 E2 E1

3. This exercise uses your second and third fingers on each of the strings.

G2 G3 G2   D2 D3 D2   A2 A3 A2   E2 E3 E2

4. This exercise uses your third and fourth fingers.

G3 G4 G3   D3 D4 D3   A3 A4 A3   E3 E4 E3

5. Here is another short piece for you to play. It requires all four fingers on the bottom two strings.

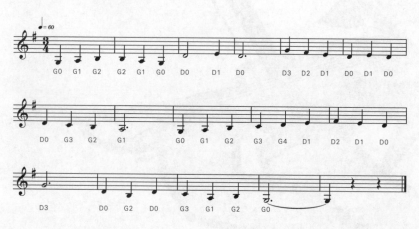

G0 G1 G2 G2 G1 G0   D0 D1 D0   D3 D2 D1 D0 D1 D0

D0 G3 G2 G1   G0 G1 G2 G3 G4 D1   D2 D1 D0

D3   D0 G2 D0   G3 G1 G2 G0

PROBLEM?

You might not always get the sound that you were expecting from your violin. Tuning can be hard on the violin because we don't have any marks on the fingerboard to show us where to put our fingers. Just adjust your finger if it sounds wrong: slide it towards you if you think it is not high enough and away from you if it is not low enough.

TEST

QUESTION 1

If you try to play a C (second finger on A), and it sounds too high, which way do you move your finger to make it lower?

QUESTION 2

What is the name of the note that is one semi-tone higher than F?

6. This piece uses all four fingers on the top three strings.

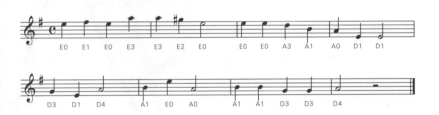

7. Now it's time to play with the piano. The recording doesn't have a tick this time because the tempo varies slightly in a few parts.

IF ALL ELSE FAILS, THERE'S ALWAYS SCALES!

Don't you go pale
At the thought of a scale.
It'll help you with your playin'…
You know what I'm sayin'?

YOUR GOALS

GOAL 1
To be able to play a major/minor scale in any key.

GOAL 2
To understand the concept of tones and semi-tones.

GOAL 3
To understand what key signatures are.

THEORY

There are many different types of scales, but the first two that we're going to look at are the most basic: the major scale and the minor scale. By listening, you can tell the difference between major and minor scales. One way of distinguishing between the two is to remember that the major tends to sound happy, and the minor sounds sad.

Every major scale consists of tones and semi-tones in this order:

Key-note, tone, tone, semi-tone, tone, tone, tone, semi-tone

On a keyboard, the notes of a D major scale look like this:

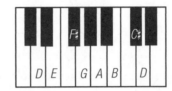

Remember, this rule applies to major scales starting on any other note. If you start on a D, the notes of a D major scale in ascending order will be as follows:

D, E, F♯, G, A, B, C♯ D

A lot of music is composed in particular 'keys'. Sometimes a composer might write a piece in the key of D major for a few bars, and then they might change ('modulate') to another key. The key of D major has two sharps (F♯ and C♯). The term used to describe the key of a piece of music is 'key signature'. The key signature can be written at different points in the music to help the player understand which notes are sharp and which are flat.

Here are all of the different major keys with their corresponding key signatures:

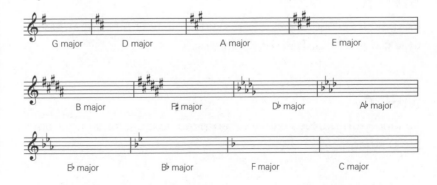

TIP

Try to always co-ordinate your bow with the action of your left fingers. This means placing your finger on the string exactly when you change bows. (Changing bows is the term that string players use when you change from an up-bow to a down-bow or vice versa). If you practise your scales slowly at first, you have more time to think about how and where you are going to put your finger down while your bow is moving.

There are two variations of the minor scale: harmonic minor and melodic minor. We are going to look at the harmonic minor, which consists of tones and semi-tones in this order:

Key-note, tone, semi-tone, tone, tone, semi-tone, tone + semi-tone, semi-tone

Notice how the sixth degree of this scale is a tone + semi-tone. That could also be measured as three semi-tones, or one-and-a-half tones. The notes of a D minor harmonic minor scale are as follows:

IN PRACTICE

Now you can try playing these scales on your violin. Start with a scale of G major.

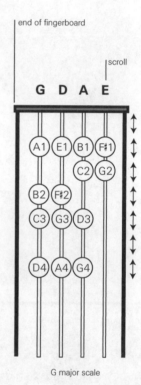
end of fingerboard

scroll

G major scale

STEP 1

Pick up your bow, like I showed you in Lesson 2, and play a down-bow on the G string.

STEP 2

Keep the bow still at the point whilst you position your first finger for the next note of the scale. Place your first finger in its first position (about a finger's width away from the nut). Now play an up-bow. This should sound as an A.

STEP 3

Place your second finger a tone away from your first finger. Now play a down-bow. This should sound a B.

STEP 4

Continue this process until you reach the next G (third finger on the D string).

EXERCISES

The following exercises will develop the idea we've just looked at, to include chromatic scales (which move up and down in semi-tones, covering ALL of the notes), and arpeggios (patterns that consist of the first, third and fifth notes of the scale).

When, in the chromatic scale, I ask you to play two consecutive notes with the same finger, gently slide between the notes.

1. This exercise shows you how to play a chromatic scale starting on G.

G0 G1—G1 G2—G2 G3 G4 D0 D1—D1 D2—D2 D3 D4 A0 A1—A1 A2—A2 A3 A4 E0 E1—E1 E2

2. This scale is a G major arpeggio.

G0 G2 D0 D3 . A1 A3 E2 A3 A1 D3 D0 G2 G0

3. This is another arpeggio starting on G, but this time it is G minor. This means that all the Bs are flattened to B flats (B♭).

G0 G2 D0 D3 A1 A3 E2 A3 A1 D3 D0 G2 G0

TEST

QUESTION 1
How can you tell the difference between a major and a minor scale just by listening?

QUESTION 2
Which notes are sharp in the key of E major?

SLUR IT

Fiddlers must learn to slur
Like cats must learn to purr
To prove that you're no fool
Slur and play it cool.

THEORY

In musical terms, to 'slur' is to play more than one note in the same bow (for a string player), more than one note to one syllable (for a singer), and more than one note to a breath (for a wind player). On the violin, slurring can be used to make the music more flowing and less disjointed. In notation, a slur is written like this:

The notes that should be slurred together are the notes that are covered by the curved line. To play a slur, the bow must travel in the same direction, and should not stop, between notes.

Another effect that composers have been using for centuries is the 'trill'. This term is used for the action of slurring two consecutive notes together and repeating them. A trill could be written out like this:

However, they are simplified like this:

Similar to a trill is a 'mordent'. Basically, mordents are small trills, and are used a lot in folk music. This is how a mordent would be written in full:

But they are usually simplified using this symbol, above or below the note:

YOUR GOALS

GOAL 1
To be able to 'slur' more than one note in the same bow.

GOAL 2
To be able to 'slur' notes across the string.

GOAL 3
To be able to 'trill'.

IN PRACTICE

PART 1: PLAYING A SLUR

STEP 1

Play an open A string with a down-bow. Start at the heel of the bow, and, when you get to the middle of the bow, stop and leave the bow where it is.

STEP 2

Place your first finger in its first position and start the bow moving again in the direction of a down-bow. Try it again and again, until you can do it without stopping the bow. The two notes should eventually flow seamlessly together.

PART 2: PLAYING A TRILL

STEP 1

Do the same as Part 1, but use hardly any bow for each note. If you start on the A string, try playing 'ABABABAB'. See how many you can get in one bow. Start slowly and gradually get faster!

PART 3: SLURRING NOTES OVER THE STRINGS

STEP 1

Place your bow at the heel on the G string and play a quarter of a down-bow.

STEP 2

Without taking your bow off the string, move your right arm slightly downwards, so that the bow hair is touching the D string. Again, play a quarter of a down-bow on the D string.

STEP 3

Follow the same procedure on the A string and the E string. You should use your last quarter of bow on the E string and should be at the tip of the bow.

STEP 4

You can now go back the other way, repeating the E for a quarter of the bow, then A, D, and finally G.

STEP 5

Repeat this process slowly, without stopping the bow, gradually getting faster.

TIP

Always keep the bow moving when you play a slur. If you are slurring across the string, make sure that the level of your bow arm is smoothly adjusted from string to string.

PROBLEM?

You might find that your bow sometimes moves too near the bridge and makes a scratchy sound. Don't worry, there are lots of new things to concentrate on so it's only natural. Just do things slowly at first so you can keep an eye on everything at once!

EXERCISES

1. This exercise teaches you how to slur two notes together. It only uses the open A string and your first finger.

2. This exercise teaches you how to play a trill. It starts with crotchets slurred together. These turn into quavers, then semi-quavers, and eventually you can try moving your fingers as fast as you can – a trill!

3. This exercise teaches you to slur notes from one string to another. Use your whole bow at the beginning, and then less and less as the notes get faster.

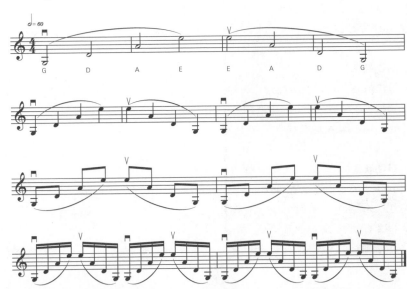

TEST

QUESTION 1
What is the term we use to describe repeated, consecutive, slurred notes that are played very fast?

QUESTION 2
What term do we use to describe when we play more than one note in the same bow without stopping?

VIBRATO

If you wanna make it sing
Then you've gotta do this thing
Make your fingers vibrate
And then just wait
'Cos the sound you'll produce
Will have a lot of use
In making sweet music
You'll never ever lose it

YOUR GOALS

GOAL 1
To know how to play
with vibrato.

GOAL 2
To be able to practise
vibrato without tensing
the left hand.

GOAL 3
To learn some exercises
that make vibrato seem
like a breeze.

THEORY

OK, so vibrato – what does this mean? Well, it's something us fiddlers
use to add depth to the sound we produce. Many musicians use some
form of vibrato. It just means that the sound wave is disturbed and the
note produced is less pure. On the violin, vibrato is achieved by subtly
adjusting the pitch of the note up and down.

You can vary the speed and width of vibrato to make different sounds.
Vibrato is a very important tool in creating an identity for individual
players. Because every single player has different-sized/-shaped fingers,
no single player is ever going to sound the same. Isn't that cool? It's a
bit like musical handwriting!

IN PRACTICE

Now, this isn't gonna be easy, so you have to be patient. Vibrato's a bit like riding a bike. It might take a while to perfect, but once you can do it, you'll never forget!

Throughout the steps described below, you need to be constantly playing up- and down-bows

STEP 1

Put your second finger on any string.

STEP 2

Roll your finger towards your body, so the note that you play is sharpened.

STEP 3

Roll your finger back, away from your body, and rest on the original note for a couple of seconds.

STEP 4

Then roll your finger in the opposite direction, away from you, flattening the note.

STEP 5

Continue doing this process, sharpening and flattening the note. It'll sound quite weird – maybe like an ambulance siren? Anyway, this is just an exercise, so don't worry! Once you get used to this, start doing it faster, gradually making the width that you are rolling your finger smaller. As soon as you start getting tense, stop and have a rest and start again slowly.

PROBLEM?

Vibrato on the violin can be tricky to learn. It can take ages because it is an action that you probably won't have ever come across before. Try not to get frustrated – when you do get the hang of it, you'll feel as if you were born with the ability to do it! Don't panic if the sound that you're making resembles a goat! This will soon improve!

TIP

Always listen carefully to the sounds you are making. Try to remember the sounds you like and how you achieve them. There is not one set way of playing the violin. You have to find the way that works best for yourself. Sometimes, our ears are prone to being lazy. It is likely that if you listen to the sounds that you are producing, and like those sounds, other people will like them, too!

EXERCISES

1. This exercise should help you develop a good vibrato. Start with your second finger on the A string and play a C. Roll your finger towards you so the note is sharpened. Roll it back to the C, and then roll it away from you to make the note flatter. Repeat this process, with as many or as few bows as you want. You can get the right idea from the CD.

2. This is the same as before but on the E string.

3. This time attempt the same exercise on the D string.

You can practise this exercise with any finger on any string.

TEST

QUESTION 1
What happens to the pitch of a note when we add vibrato?

QUESTION 2
What are three other musical instruments that use vibrato?

MAGICAL VIOLIN MYSTERIES REVEALED...

There are so many wicked sounds you can make with your violin. You can make your listeners feel happy, sad, scared, confused, excited, bored, lonely, lost, in love – that is the beauty of music.

THEORY

As a musician, one thing you can do to vary the sound of your music is to play at different volumes. There are a range of terms that composers and musicians use to describe how loud they want you to play. These directions are called 'dynamics'.

ABBREVIATION	ITALIAN NAME	VOLUME
pp	(Pianissimo)	Very quiet
p	(Piano)	Quiet
mp	(Mezzo piano)	Fairly quiet
mf	(Mezzo forte)	Fairly loud
f	(Forte)	Loud
ff	(Fortissimo)	Very loud

Composers often use the Italian term 'crescendo' when they want the sound to get louder. They use the Italian term 'diminuendo' when they want the sound to get quieter. We also use symbols that we call 'hairpins' to show crescendos and diminuendos. The hairpins are placed beneath the notes that the composer wishes to affect.

In the diagram below, the hairpin directs the music to start quietly, get louder and then get quieter again. The loudest note is the third finger on A.

There are so many different sounds that you can get from your violin… I am going to tell you how to make a few of them and I want you to experiment with weird and wonderful techniques. (This doesn't include trying to play it underwater or whilst doing a headstand! Ya get me?!)

One thing that composers sometimes ask for is called 'ponticello' in Italian or 'sul pont' in French. This means 'on the bridge'. You can do this by bowing really, really close to the bridge. It should make an eerie, scratchy sound. Cool, eh?

Another direction that composers sometimes use is 'tremolo'. This Italian word means a rapid succession of up- and down-bows. Depending on the speed and dynamic of the tremolo, it can create many different effects.

IN PRACTICE

STEP 1

Play an open E down-bow and see how much you can make the string vibrate. The more it vibrates, the better the sound will be. To make a loud sound (forte), you can use your bow in a variety of ways. Speed and pressure of the bow against the string will affect how loud the sound will be.

STEP 2

To play quietly (piano), you can use less pressure/less speed of the bow against the strings. Either of these things will make the sound quieter. To get different sounds, you can do one or the other or even both of these things!

STEP 3

Now you can try starting quietly on one note and getting louder.
Try starting with a slow bow with not very much pressure and
gradually let it get faster and increase the pressure. It is actually
more natural to start quietly at the point and get louder towards
the heel, and vice versa.

STEP 4

Try playing sul pont/ponticello. Place the bow really close to the
bridge and play any notes that you want.

STEP 5

Now try playing tremolo (♪). This is more effective at the tip of
the bow. Start about 10cm away from the tip and play a down-
bow open E. Then play an up-bow E, so the bow is back 10cm
from the tip. Keep making these small bows, and gradually get
faster and faster.

EXERCISES

1. This exercise is composed with different dynamics. Follow the music
and play the dynamics that I have written.

2. This exercise is for practising getting louder and softer. Start with
a slow speed of bow and light pressure against the strings, and, as
the hairpin directs you to get louder, use a faster bow with greater
pressure.

3. This exercise is for practising sul pont/ponticello, playing with your
bow very close to the bridge.

4. This exercise is for practising tremolo. It only uses open strings.

TIP

Try all of these tricks at different volumes. Ponticello, for example, can sound really mysterious and chilling when you play it quietly, but, as soon as you exert greater pressure, it becomes very harsh and scary.

PROBLEM?

It isn't easy to stay relaxed when you try to do tremolo – especially when you do it very fast. Try not to raise your shoulder, and be aware of the feeling in your forearm muscles. You should use a combination of your wrist and your arm when you do this.

TEST

QUESTION 1
What is the Italian term for playing near the bridge?

QUESTION 2
What is the Italian term for rapid, successive up- and down-bows?

QUESTION 3
What is the Italian term for playing very quietly?

TWO AT A TIME

One of the many wicked things about the violin is that it can play more than one note at the same time. Most wind instruments aren't capable of doing this. On string instruments this technique is called 'double-stopping'. It's like playing chords on the guitar or piano, and means that we have endless possibilities of different harmonies. We can accompany ourselves!

In this lesson, don't you see
You're gonna learn sweet harmony
People will be saying
'Bout the chords you'll be playing
Listen to that sound
Yo! That sound is round!

THEORY

There are many types of 'double-stopping'. To 'stop' a note on the violin is to put your finger on the string. You can play chords with varying combinations of open strings and stopped notes. Below are some examples of different types of double-stops.

An example of when one note is an 'open' string and one is 'stopped':

An example of when both notes are 'stopped':

A four-note chord that can be 'spread', ie the bottom two notes played at the same time, followed by the top two:

The bridge of the violin is curved so that we can play single notes without disturbing the other strings. That is why we have to 'spread' chords of more than two notes.

YOUR GOALS

GOAL 1
To be able to play one or more notes at the same time.

GOAL 2
To be able to play an open-string drone whilst playing a tune on the adjacent string.

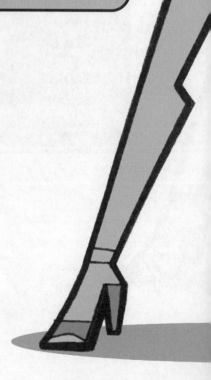

IN PRACTICE

PART 1: OPEN-STRING & ONE 'STOPPED' NOTE

STEP 1
Play an open G.

STEP 2
Carry on bowing the G string whilst you position your first finger on the D string to play an E.

STEP 3
Once the finger is in position, adjust your right elbow slightly towards the floor so that the bow is playing both the strings.

PART 2: BOTH NOTES STOPPED

STEP 1
Position your first finger on the A string and play a B.

STEP 2
Continue playing this note whilst you position your second finger on the E string.

STEP 3
Bring your elbow down slightly so that the bow is touching both strings. You should be playing both notes.

PART 3: A FOUR-NOTE CHORD

STEP 1
Position your first finger in the same positions as in Part 2. (First finger positioned on B on the A string and second finger positioned on G on the E string)

STEP 2
Position your bow at the heel, touching both the G and D strings.

STEP 3
Slowly play these two notes until you get to the middle of the bow. While you are playing them, let your right arm move downwards, so that your bow is positioned over the top two strings, and use the rest of the bow to play this double-stop.

Practise this procedure slowly at first. When you feel comfortable with it, you should be able to play it faster.

TIP
To make both the strings vibrate and make the sound that you desire, you need to keep an eye on your bow to ensure that it is always in the right position (touching both the strings that you want to double-stop), and that it is always moving horizontally to the bridge.

PROBLEM?

Chords are sometimes hard to tune because you are having to focus on more than one note at a time. When you are practising them, start with one note, and once you are happy with the tuning and the sound, add the next note and tune it to the first note. The distance between specific notes is called an 'interval'. Some intervals in chords will be easier to tune than others. An octave is a good interval to practise tuning because the notes should sound the same as each other.

TEST

QUESTION 1
Why can't we play four notes simultaneously on the violin?

QUESTION 2
What is the term we use to describe playing more than one note at a time?

QUESTION 3
What is the English term that we use to describe the distance between two notes?

EXERCISES

1. This exercise concentrates on how to double-stop an 'open-string' and a 'stopped' note.

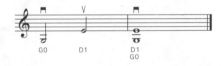

G0   D1   D1
          G0

2. This exercise shows you how to play two 'stopped' notes.

A1   E2   E2
          A1

E2   A1   E2
          A1

3. This exercise focuses on how to play a four-note chord.

IMPROVISING

In this lesson, you're gonna soothe people with your wicked groove. Making up stuff isn't tough; just don't be shy, it's easy as pie!

Improvising is all about playing something without preparation – without all the notes being written down in advance. It's wicked because it means that you are free to play exactly what you feel at the time. There are certain types of music where improvisation is used more than others. Jazz musicians improvise a lot. I am going to teach you a few scales so that you can improvise with some cool musicians on the CD.

YOUR GOALS

GOAL 1
To be able to follow a sequence of chords played by some jazz musicians.

GOAL 2
To be able to improvise in different modes and keys.

THEORY

Improvising can take many different forms. It is possible to improvise on your own, or with other players, without deciding anything beforehand. However, often when musicians improvise together, they decide on a series of chords over which they will play their own lines. In the previous lesson, you will hopefully have experimented playing different chords on your violin. Some will have been pleasant, and perhaps some may have sounded a bit freaky. When you have a structure to improvise to, you can decide when you want notes to sound nice and when you want them to sound weird. Sometimes weird chords make the nicer ones sound even better, and vice versa!

In this lesson, I am going to teach you a series of scales that will go with the chords the jazz musicians are playing on the CD.

TIP
If you learn these scales and become familiar with the chord structure of the piece, eventually you will be able to play along without the music.

PROBLEM?

You might find that sometimes you lose track of where you are in the music. Don't worry, just keep cool and always remember that you're playing an instrument that can do almost anything. There are millions of sound effects that you can play with until you find your place!

EXERCISES

1. Firstly, practise playing each of the scales written below.

F minor dorian

Ab dominant 7th

D minor dorian

Eventually, you will be able to play along to the track using whichever notes of these scales that you desire. Some notes will work better than others and, the great thing is, you can be as simple or as complicated as you like – it's totally up to you!

2. Listen to the next track on the CD to get a feel for the music. The tempo of the track is given at the beginning by the metronome. There are four beats in a bar and, if you follow the music, you will see that each chord lasts for four bars. When the chord changes you can play notes using the next scale.

TRACK 39

TRACK 40

TRACK 41

TRACK 42

TEST

QUESTION 1

What are the notes of the F minor dorian scale?

QUESTION 2

Can you can learn all of the scales that I have shown you and the symbols of the chords that they are based on?

TOP 10 ARTISTS

JEAN-LUC PONTY

Jean-Luc Ponty was originally trained classically, studying the violin at the Paris Conservatoire. His interest in jazz developed while he was playing tenor sax in a band. He learned the rules of jazz and how to improvise, and soon started playing jazz on his violin. Two of his greatest heroes were John Coltrane and Miles Davis. These influences can be heard in Jean-Luc's playing, his phrasing and pure sound (without vibrato) being similar to a trumpeter's. When his career started to kick off, critics of the time considered him to be the only jazz violinist as exciting as a saxophonist!

He experimented a lot with electro-acoustics and was successful in liberating the violin from stereotypes. Frank Zappa was intrigued by Jean-Luc's musical imagination and asked him to join him and his band, The Mothers Of Invention, with whom the violinist toured for seven months.

Jean-Luc has enjoyed a very colourful career, performing with a number of amazing musicians, including Stuff Smith, Stéphane Grappelli and Sir Elton John!

STATISTICS

DATE OF BIRTH
29 September 1942

PLACE OF BIRTH
Avranches, France

INFLUENCES
John Coltrane, Miles Davis

FIRST ALBUM
Jazz Long Playing (1964)

LISTEN TO

Jazz Long Playing
King Kong
Honky Chateau
Tchokola

IN THE STYLE OF...

TRACK 46

Jean-Luc has a very distinctive sound, which has helped make his career interesting and varied, playing with the likes of Frank Zappa. He hardly uses vibrato and his sound is often quite edgy and direct.

NICCOLO PAGANINI

Niccolò Paganini's father insisted that he started learning the violin when he was seven years old. When he reached the age of 13, the boy went to Parma, Italy, to have more violin lessons. The teachers there were so astonished by his playing that they felt they could not teach him anything else. So, he began teaching himself and would often lock himself in his room and practise for 15 hours at a time!

His technique was unlike any other violinist before him. His concerts were always sold out, not only because he could play with amazing agility and flair, but also because he captivated his audiences with his ability to make melodies speak. He composed a lot of music and performed mainly his own compositions in concerts. His '24 Caprices For Solo Violin' are very popular today and are still considered to be some of the most difficult pieces in the violin repertoire!

Many people were intrigued by Paganini's appearance. It was commonly thought by audiences that he had sold his soul to the Devil for his exceptional skills on the violin. He did nothing to try to deny such rumours. Indeed, he would dress his gaunt, spindly frame in black, from head to toe, and he would arrive at concerts in a black coach drawn by black horses.

STATISTICS

DATE OF BIRTH
27 October 1782

DIED
27 May 1840

STARTED VIOLIN
Seven years old

MOST POPULAR COMPOSITION
'24 Caprices For Solo Violin'

IN THE STYLE OF...

Paganini composed loads of music to show off his incredible technique. Unfortunately, because he died a long time ago, there are no recordings of his playing. However, you can imagine that he would have played with great confidence and flair! Try to bring out those traits in the following example…

TRACK 45 CD

SUPERSTAR TIP!

In concert, Paganini would amaze audiences with imaginative tricks on his violin. He would occasionally play so loud and so high that his top three strings would snap and he'd continue the rest of the piece on the G string!

TRUE STORY!

Paganini was riddled with different diseases throughout his life. One ailment that was actually advantageous to the virtuoso violinist was called 'Ehlers-Danlos', a syndrome that caused excessively flexible joints. This meant that he could stretch his fingers to reach intervals far greater than other violinists could.

NATALIE MACMASTER

Natalie MacMaster comes from Cape Breton, Canada. The town has a strong tradition of folk music derived from the forefathers of Cape Bretoners, who emigrated from Scotland centuries ago, bringing with them traditional Scottish folk music. Natalie's music combines Celtic traditional acoustic instruments (fiddle, piano and bagpipes) with modern instruments (electric guitars and synthesisers). Her latest album combines bluegrass and Celtic music, and she recorded this with established bluegrass musicians Bella Fleck, Jerry Douglas, Sam Bush and Edgar Meyer.

STATISTICS

PLACE OF BIRTH
Cape Breton, Canada

AGE STARTED VIOLIN
Nine years old

MEMORABLE GIGS
Has shared stages with Carlos Santana, The Chieftains, Paul Simon and Luciano Pavarotti

IN THE STYLE OF...

TRACK 46

CD

SUPERSTAR TIP!

Natalie hosts her own radio show in Cape Breton every Saturday night on CBC. Well, that's one way to guarantee that people hear your music!

TRUE STORY!

Natalie was encouraged to play the fiddle by her great uncle, Buddy MacMaster, who is a very famous Cape Breton fiddler and has been a great influence and help to Natalie.

Natalie's music is modern Scottish folk. She has a beautiful, clear tone and uses a modest amount of vibrato. This piece is characterised by dotted rhythms and mordents, both of which feature highly in Natalie's music.

VANESSA MAE

Vanessa Mae started playing the violin at the tender age of five, a year after moving to London from Singapore. It was not long before she started to shine, and she made her first professional public appearance at the age of ten with The Philharmonica Orchestra in London. She impressed audiences worldwide with her interpretation of classical concertos and virtuoso showpieces. However, it was not this repertoire that would make Vanessa Mae a household name. In 1995, she released her first 'crossover' album. She pioneered a new type of classic/pop fusion music that still proves to be popular across the globe.

Vanessa Mae's spectacular concerts have become increasingly diverse over the years. As well as playing the violin in her shows, she also dances and sings.

STATISTICS

DATE OF BIRTH
27 October 1978

PLACE OF BIRTH
Singapore

FIRST HIT SINGLE
'Toccata And Fugue In D Minor'. This reworking of JS Bach's masterpiece reached #14 in the UK singles chart

FIRST HIT ALBUM
The Violin Player (1995) was the album from which 'Toccata And Fugue' was taken. It stayed in the UK pop album charts for several months

INSTRUMENTS USED
Guadagnini violin (made in 1761)
Hill violin (made in 1860)
Zeta electric violins

LISTEN TO

The Violin Player
Storm
Choreography

IN THE STYLE OF...

Vanessa Mae started off playing classical violin. You can still see this in her playing today, but she has also developed her own unique style. She is very elegant when she plays, and her bow-arm particularly stands out as being very precise. She also dances when she plays. You can try this, too!

EOS CHATER

Eos is the second violinist in the sensational all-girl string quartet Bond. She studied at The Royal College Of Music with Dona Lee Croft. While she was at college, she played with many bands including The Divine Comedy and The Cocteau Twins. Eos is originally from Cardiff, Wales.

Bond generally play with a group of session musicians (drums, guitar and bass), and their shows are always live. They were the source of controversy when they were 'kicked out' of the Classical Charts when they entered at #2.

Each member of Bond has written music on each of the albums so far. Eos has always been a keen composer and has a very eclectic musical taste. She loves funky pop/electronica by the likes of Daft Punk and Goldfrapp. She also likes music by minimalist composers such as Steve Reich and Philip Glass. Two of the pieces she has written for Bond which you can look out for are 'Ride' and 'Midnight Garden'.

STATISTICS

DATE OF BIRTH
27 January 1976

PLACE OF BIRTH
Cardiff, Wales

INFLUENCES
Dona Lee Croft (her violin teacher), Donny Hathaway, Scott Walker, Daft Punk, Goldfrapp

INSTRUMENT OF CHOICE
Starfish electric violin

LISTEN TO

Shine
Classified

IN THE STYLE OF...

TRUE STORY!

Last year, Bond were playing at the *GQ* Man Of The Year Awards in New York. There were loads of famous people there, including Lenny Kravitz, Keifer Sutherland, Hugh Grant, Denzel Washington and Naomi Campbell. There wasn't time for a rehearsal beforehand, so they were only told about the set-up of the stage. When it came to their time to play on stage, the wind machines started doing their thing... Eos was wearing a floaty dress and when she realised that this might have been a bad move, she started signalling to the stage-hands to turn the fans down. They misinterpreted her signs and turned the machines up, giving the star-studded audience an eyeful!

Eos was classically trained, so she has a very assured technique. She loves trying to find new sounds, so why don't you experiment when you play along to this next song? The first time through, you will hear the first and second violin parts. The second time, the second part will be cut, so you can play it on your own with the first violin.

TRACK 48

SHARON CORR

Sharon Corr is a member of Irish pop/Celtic sensation The Corrs. The band is made up of her brother, Jim, and her two sisters, Andrea and Caroline. As a pop group, they are illuminated by the fact that they write their own material, co-produce their own records and play their own instruments. Sharon is the band's violinist, one of its vocalists and is also a composer and songwriter. She enchants audiences with her gentle manner and the beautiful, wistful sound that she makes on her violin.

STATISTICS

DATE OF BIRTH
24 March 1970

PLACE OF BIRTH
Dundalk, Co Lough, Ireland

DEBUT ALBUM
Forgiven Not Forgotten

STARTED VIOLIN
Six years old

LISTEN TO

In Bloom (2000)
Talk On Corners (1999)
Forgiven Not Forgotten (1996)

IN THE STYLE OF...

TRUE STORY!

The siblings formed a band so that they could audition for the 1991 Irish film *The Commitments*, by Alan Parker. Consequently, all four of them successfully gained small parts in the film. The musical director, John Hughes, realised the family's musical potential and decided that he wanted to manage them.

Sharon is a very elegant violinist. She always stands with beautiful posture and great poise. The tune that I have written in Sharon's style has a violin solo at the beginning that I think would suit Sharon very well. It is quite lively and has a definite Irish/folky flavour!

STEPHANE GRAPPELLI

Stéphane Grappelli is probably the most famous jazz violinist who ever lived. His improvising was incredible, and his sound sweet and colourful. One memorable occasion was when he joined Jean-Luc Ponty, Stuff Smith and Svend Asmussen at the Violin Summit in Basle, Switzerland, in 1964. In the early '70s, he appeared on UK TV alongside Yehudi Menuhin, playing jazz duets. The most important springboard for his career was his appearance with Diz Disley and Denny Wright at the 1973 UK Cambridge Folk Festival. His playing was unbelievable and, because of this amazing performance, he became hot jazz property and toured the world for the next two decades, performing in the best venues to the biggest audiences.

STATISTICS

DATE OF BIRTH
26 January 1908

PLACE OF BIRTH
Paris, France

DATE OF DEATH
1 December 1997

IMPORTANT INFLUENCES
Django Rheinhardt (guitarist), Diz Disley

LISTEN TO

Collection
Happy Reunion
I Got The Whole World On A String

IN THE STYLE OF...

Grappelli's sound is very distinctive. Many of his recordings are very chirpy and bouncy. The sound of his bow against the strings gives a sense of lightness and his vibrato is SO sweet!

YEHUDI MENUHIN

Menuhin grew up in New York and was a distinguished violinist at a very early age. He found fame at the tender age of seven with his performance of the Elgar Violin Concerto. His playing has always been remarkable, with a deep sense of understanding that set him aside from other virtuosi. Menuhin studied with George Enesco in Paris and he remained a close friend and influence on him for the rest of his life.

In 1963, Menuhin opened the Yehudi Menuhin School, a school for musically gifted children. This school is still thriving and has produced some of the greatest musicians of this century. Menuhin collaborated with Ravi Shankar, the great Indian composer and sitarist, in 1967, and they recorded an album called *West Meets East*. The fusing together of the stereotypical soundworlds from each of these geographically and culturally distant countries was revolutionary. The sound of sitar, tanpura and tabla is beautifully interwoven with the sweet sonority of the violin.

In the last 20 years of his life, Menuhin started conducting and worked with many great orchestras around the world. He did a lot of work for charity and was an important spokesperson for many causes.

STATISTICS

DATE OF BIRTH
22 April 1916

DATE OF DEATH
12 March 1999

PLACE OF BIRTH
New York

INFLUENCES
George Enesco, Wilhelm Furtwängler

SUCCESSFUL COLLABORATIONS
Stéphane Grappelli, Ravi Shankar

LISTEN TO

Bach: Sonatas And Partitas For Solo Violin (1957–58)
Pieces De Virtuosite
West Meets East

IN THE STYLE OF...

SUPERSTAR TIP!

During the '40s and '50s, Menuhin performed a number of lesser-known works and opened many windows for performers of this time. He commissioned the composer Béla Bartók to write 'Sonata for Solo Violin', and was the first artist to perform this demanding work. His interpretation impressed Bartók greatly, and violinists today still refer to this recording with admiration.

TRUE STORY!

After World War II, Menuhin played his violin to hundreds of recently released prisoners of war from the concentration camps in Germany.

Menuhin's playing will always be remembered for his musicality and dedication to the music. This piece below is a light-hearted, 'Kreisler'-esque kind of piece, which I think would have suited Menuhin very well. I think he would have played it with lots of character and swing, so make sure you do too!

JOSHUA BELL

Joshua was born and brought up in Bloomington, Indiana, USA. So far in his career, Joshua has been successful playing in many different styles. These include classical recordings and concerts, and some very exciting cross-over projects. He has collaborated with three incredible Bluegrass musicians (double-bassist Edgar Meyer, guitarist Mike Marshall, mandolinist Sam Bush), and also recorded the soundtrack for the critically acclaimed film, *The Red Violin*, starring Samuel L Jackson. The film tells the story of a violin and follows its path through centuries of different masters, triumphs and tragedies.

STATISTICS

PLACE OF BIRTH
Bloomington, Indiana, USA

SPECIAL ACHIEVEMENTS
Grammy nominations for *Short Trip Home, Gershwin Fantasy, The Red Violin* and *Listen To The Storyteller*

INSTRUMENT OF CHOICE
Antonius Stradivarius (made in 1713)

FAVOURITE TV APPEARANCE
Sesame Street

IN THE STYLE OF...

This composition demonstrates Joshua's wonderful, soulful sonority. He plays with a luscious vibrato. Why don't you try to emulate it here?

NIGEL KENNEDY

Nigel Kennedy has been one of the greatest violinists to come from Britain. He studied at the Menuhin School when he was young and was Lord Yehudi Menuhin's most well-known pupil. Not only is he a legendary violinist, he is a character too, and has always stood out from other classical violinists with his unusual dress sense and ever-changing punk hairstyles! His image, combined with some of the risqué music he has released, has meant that he has often been a source of controversy. He has taken part in so many different projects, ranging from recordings of many classical concertos to ones inspired by Jimi Hendrix and The Doors.

In concert, Kennedy is often unpredictable; he'll often walk straight onto the stage from his sports car (not from the dressing room like most musicians!), and one of his trademarks is high-fiving members of the audience. He is also a massive football fan and has supported Aston Villa for years!

STATISTICS

INFLUENCES
Lord Yehudi Menuhin, The Doors, Jimi Hendrix, Dorothy DeLay (his violin teacher from New York), Fritz Kreisler, Jean-Luc Ponty

MOST POPULAR RECORDING
Vivaldi's *Four Seasons* sold over two million copies. It also earned a place in *The Guiness Book Of Records* as the best-selling classical record of all time

INSTRUMENTS USED
Guarneri (made in 1736 by Giuseppe Guarneri del Gesu in Cremona, Italy)

LISTEN TO

The Doors Concerto **(2000)** *Sibelius Violin Concerto –* **Conducted by Simon Rattle with the City of Birmingham Symphony Orchestra** *Nigel Kennedy Plays Jazz*

IN THE STYLE OF...

Many people associate Nigel Kennedy with Vivaldi's 'The Four Seasons' because it's one of his biggest hits to date. The piece I have written for you to play is inspired by Kennedy's performance of 'The Four Seasons'. To play this piece in the style of Kennedy, you have to play it in a very authoritative way. If you feel like stamping occasionally as it gets louder, go ahead! I've seen Kennedy do it!

TRACK 53 CD

SUPERSTAR TIP!

Nigel has always been a very hard worker and he has such diverse tastes in music that he always surprises his audiences. Because of this, he has many devoted fans across the world! Proof that a varied repertoire can only be a good thing!

TRUE STORY!

As a young man, Nigel studied in New York with a very well-known teacher, Dorothy DeLay. She often told him not to play jazz violin and to stick to classical. However, he was friends with Stéphane Grappelli and was invited to play up on stage at Carnegie Hall. This got back to his teacher and she told him that he'd never be able to record a classical record again because of that single performance. She thought that it would ruin his reputation and that people wouldn't be able to take him seriously after that. How wrong she turned out to be!

NOTES

NOTES

NOTES

GLOSSARY

ADJUSTERS
Metal screws that can vary the pitches of the strings. Positioned on tail piece and can be used for fine-tuning.

CRESCENDO
Italian term for getting louder.

DIMINUENDO
Italian term for getting quieter.

DOWN-BOW
When the bow moves from the heel to the point.

FORTISSIMO
Italian term for very loud.

PIZZICATO
Italian term for plucking.

KEY SIGNATURE
The number of sharps or flats in a key.

OCTAVE
This is the interval between two notes that are seven diatonic scale degrees (five tones and two semi-tones) apart.

PERNAMBUCO
Tree that grows in northeastern Brazil. The Pernambuco wood is the most suitable wood for bow-making. It is naturally resilient and is reddish-brown in colour.

PIANISSIMO
Italian term for very quiet.

PONTICELLO
Italian term for playing on or near the bridge.

TUNING PEGS
Wooden pegs positioned in the pegbox. They can be used to regulate the pitches of the strings.

ROSIN
String players rub rosin on their bow hair to provide friction. Made from the distillation of the oil of turpentine, rosin is moulded into blocks.

SLUR
When two or more notes are played in the same direction of the bow, without stopping the sound.

SUL PONT
French for playing on or near the bridge.

TEMPO
The speed of a composition. Often composers indicate the tempo with metronome markings. This is measured by the number of beats per minute (BPM).

TREMOLO
Rapid repetition of a note (with the bow).

TRILL
Rapid repetition of two adjacent notes in a slur.

UP-BOW
When the bow moves from the point to the heel.

VIBRATO
Oscillation of the pitch of a note.

ANSWERS TO TEST QUESTIONS

LESSON 1

1. E
2. Pizzicato
3. Away from you

LESSON 2

1. Down-bow
2. Pernambuco
3. Rosin

LESSON 3

1. Rest
2. Semi-quaver, quaver, crotchet, minim, semi-breve, dotted

LESSON 4

1. Away from you
2. F♯

LESSON 5

1. Major = happy, minor = sad

LESSON 6

1. Trill
2. Slur

LESSON 7

1. Pitch subtly adjusted up and down
2. Voice, saxophone, guitar

LESSON 8

1. Ponticello
2. Tremolo
3. Pianissimo

LESSON 9

1. Bridge is curved so the bow can't touch all the strings at the same time
2. Double-stop
3. Interval

LESSON 10

1. F minor dorian scale
2. G A♭ B♭ C D E♭ F